INVESTIGATIVE EXPERIMENTAL
ORGANIC CHEMISTRY
Microscale Approach

Nyenty Arrey, Ph.D.

Capital University, Columbus, Ohio

Linus
Publications, Inc.

Published by Linus Publications, Inc.
Deer Park, NY 11729

ISBN: 1-60797-186-0

Printed in the United States of America.

Print Numbers   5   4   3   2   1

TABLE OF CONTENTS

PREFACE

Philosophy behind Organic Chemistry Laboratory II.

Traditionally, sophomore organic chemistry laboratory have been performed in such a way that most of the students don't really understand the chemistry behind the experiments. Students have basically used their laboratory textbook as a cookbook. As a result of this, we have decided to approach the laboratory experiments in an investigative manner. Most of the experiments are adapted from published organic chemistry laboratory textbooks. The objectives of this Guided Inquiry-Base organic chemistry laboratory are:

1. to direct students to the literature;

2. to encourage students to apply their knowledge to the topics covered in lecture;

3. to promote chemical problem solving;

4. to enhance their critical thinking skills;

5. to make the students interact with their peers, teaching assistants and the instructors.

To Our Students

We hope that this exercise is going to be meaningful and rewarding to you as a method for reviewing your organic chemistry material. Please let us know what you think about this approach to organic chemistry laboratory. Remember that your honest feedback and suggestions will help us do better in the future.

Dr. L. Nyenty Arrey
Associate Professor of Chemistry

Electrophilic Aromatic Substitution: Bromination of Acetanilide

Purpose

The goal of this experiment is the determination of the product of this reaction. At the end of the experiment, you will perform the following analysis (IR,^{1}HNMR and MP) to confirm the identity of the reaction product.

Chemical Equation

Prelab Exercise: Which of three possible products result from bromination of acetanilide?

Experimental

WARNING : Bromine is a severe irritant. Wear plastic gloves when handling bromine since bromine burns can be severe and require extended periods of time to heal. Dispense bromine only in the hood.

Ref: Mayo, Pike & Trumper, *Microscale Organic Laboratory*, 4th Ed. Wiley 2000, p 330.

Weigh and place 100 mg of acetanilide in a 5.0 mL conical vial fitted with a cap. Add 16 drops of glacial acetic acid using a medicine dropper. Stirring with a glass rod may be necessary to help dissolve the acetanilide. Now add to the solution six drops of the bromine-acetic acid solution [HOOD]. Cap the vial immediately.

Allow the solution to stand at room temperature for 10 minutes with intermittent shaking. During this period, colored crystals precipitate from the solution. Next add 2.0 mL of water using a Pasteur pipet to the reaction mixture with swirling, followed by 20 drops of aqueous sodium bisulfite solution (33%). Cool the reaction mixture in an ice bath for 10 minutes to maximize the yield of product.

Collect the crystals by vacuum filtration using a Hirsch funnel (*For references relating to the use of Hirsch funnel, see Organic Chemistry Laboratory Techniques by L. Nyenty Arrey*). Wash the product with three 1 mL portions of cold water (Pasteur pipet) and partially dry; by drawing air through the crystals under reduced pressure for approximately 10 minutes.

Purify the crude product by recrystallization from 95% ethanol using the Craig tube. Weigh the dried product and calculate the percent yield. Perform the required analysis to identify your product.

Computational Chemistry (Spartan 2008 Molecular Model Program)

1. Construct a model of the intermediate(s) and the product.

2. Perform energy calculations, IR, and NMR.

3. Compare the energies between the possible intermediates.

4. Determine the percent difference of the calculated and experimental IR.

Waste Disposal

Collect all organic waste in a beaker during the experiment and dispose of the combined waste at the end of the period into the **organic waste container in the HOOD**.

Writeup

Follow the directions in the syllabus.

Experiment 1
Bromination of Acetanilide

Name: _____

Prelab Exercise: Which of three possible products results from mono-bromination of acetanilide?

Further your understanding of the chemistry in this lab by answering the following questions:

Name: _____

1. At the completion of a chemical reaction, it is common for the product to be contaminated with the starting material or products of side reactions. List three methods that could be used to determine if the product in this reaction, p-bromoacetanilide, was contaminated with acetanilide. For each method, give specific details of what you would expect to see for a pure product, and what you would expect to see for a contaminated product.

2. The reaction chemistry is explained by the role of the −NHCOCH$_3$ group which donates electron density from the nitrogen atom to the aromatic ring. Draw three other resonance structures for acetanilide that results in negative charge in the ring. Explain how the resonance structures you've drawn results in the aromatic ring being nucleophilic.

3. Propose a synthetic route for the reaction below. Show all reagents and intermediate structures for each step.

Nitration of Alkyl Benzenes

Purpose

This experiment involves nitration(HNO_3/H_2SO_4) of monosubstituted benzenes. You will perform a nitration reaction on an assigned alkyl benzene, isolate the product and determine the resulting distribution of isomers using gas chromatography. Using the knowledge of electrophilic aromatic substitution, the data gathered by the class will be analyzed to explain the various distribution of isomers.

Chemical Equation

R = methyl, ethyl,
isopropyl, or t-butyl

Prelab Exercise : How does the variation in alkyl groups influence the outcome of the nitration of alkyl benzene?

Experimental

WARNING : Be very careful with the acid reagent. It contains 66% sulfuric acid and 34% nitric acid. It can burn your skin quickly and severely. Immediately wash off any acid that spills on you for 10 minutes under running water, and clean up any spills with sodium bicarbonate solution (NaHCO$_3$) found in the safety cabinet.

Place 3.0 mL of your alkyl benzene into a 10 mL round-bottom flask using a syringe. Stir the liquid slowly using a spin vane and magnetic stirrer. Add dropwise 1 mL of nitrating reagent to the alkyl benzene and place an air condenser on the flask and stir for 20 minutes.

After 20 minutes, place the reaction flask in an ice bath and add 1.2 mL of ice cold distilled water dropwise through the top of the air condenser and continue to stir for 10 minutes *This will stop the reaction.* To the cold solution add slowly (dropwise) 2-3 mL of diethyl ether through the air condenser. **If you notice any boiling during the addition, stop adding ether and stir the mixture on ice for another 5 min.** When all the ether is added , stir the flask for another minute. Place the organic layer (ether layer, top layer, product layer, bottom layer) in a 10 mL Erlenmeyer flask using a pipet. Extract the aqueous layer again with another 1 mL of ether and combine the ether extracts (*For extraction technique, see Organic Chemistry Laboratory Techniques Manual*). Next, add 1 mL of distilled water to the ethereal extract and stir for 30 seconds. Remove the water layer, wash with another 1 mL of water and remove the water layer again.

Dry the ether layer by adding a small amount of anhydrous sodium sulfate. Let the mixture stand for a few minutes, and transfer the ether solution to a clean 10 mL Erlenmeyer flask. Wash the sodium sulfate with 0.5 mL of fresh ether to maximize product yield and transfer the ether wash to the rest of the ether solution. Evaporate the ether by placing the flask on a hot plate set between 3-4. Evaporation takes about 20 minutes and leaves the final product mixture (nitrated alkyl benzenes).

Continue with the gas chromatography analysis if there is at least 30 minutes left in the class period, otherwise schedule a time with your instructor outside of class to perform the analysis. Inject 1 uL of product into the gas chromatograph. From the resulting chromatogram, calculate the peak areas (height times width at half height) and determine the % of each isomer in your product using the formula given below.

$$\% \text{ ortho isomer} = \frac{\text{area othro isomer peak}}{\text{total area of all peaks}} * 100$$

$$\% \text{ meta isomer} = \frac{\text{area meta isomer peak}}{\text{total area of all peaks}} * 100$$

$$\% \text{ para isomer} = \frac{\text{area para isomer peak}}{\text{total area of all peaks}} * 100$$

Procedural Notes on Gas Chromatography

All of the reaction products are volatile to be analyzed using gas chromatography. The largest product peak should deflect the recorder pen at least two-thirds of the way up the chart paper, but not off the scale. You can also use the attenuation setting on the instrument to adjust the peak sizes. Lowering the attenuation setting by a factor of two will double the size of the peaks. The order of elution of the isomers is ortho first, followed by meta and para. It is common for the meta isomer peak to overlap the para isomer peak. You may also see peaks early in the chromatogram for air, acetone, ether and/or the alkyl benzene starting material.

Compare the percentages of isomers from your reaction to those of your group members. During the next lab session, we will discuss the class results to make predictions about the reactivity of other aromatic compounds.

Waste Disposal

Any waste containing ether goes into the **Organic Waste Container in the HOOD**. All aqueous waste goes down the drain with lots of water.

Writeup

Follow directions on the syllabus unless otherwise instructed.

Experiment 2
Nitration of Alkyl Benzenes

Name: ——

Prelab Exercise : How does the variation in alkyl groups influence the outcome of the nitration of alkyl benzene?

Name: ——

Answer the following questions:

1. One of the most powerful aspects of a well developed theory is the ability to use it to predict the results of future experiments. Based on the conclusions from this laboratory, predict the product(s) from nitration of p-tert-butyltoluene shown below. Explain your reasoning.

2. The original reports of this experiment (Nelson and Brown *J. Am. Chem. Soc.* **1951**, 73, 5605. Brown and Bonner, *J. Am. Chem. Soc* **1954**, 76, 605.) used distillation to separate the three mononitro isomers. The separated products were then weighed to determine the relative amount of each isomer. Give one reason why distillation is less effective for analyzing the product distribution in this experiment and gas chromatography is more effective.

Grignard Reaction:
Synthesis of an Alcohol

Important: The formation of Grignard reagents looks simple and straight forward on paper but it is challenging in the laboratory especially if the necessary precautions are not followed carefully. **Place all the glassware in the oven the day before the experiment**.

Purpose

This is a two step reaction. In the first part of the experiment a Grignard reagent is prepared from a monosubstituted halobenzene using magnesium. This Grignard reagent will be used in the second part of the synthesis by reacting it with a ketone or aldehyde to form an alcohol. The identity of the final product will be confirmed using melting point, IR, and proton NMR.

Chemical Equations

Prelab Exercise : Provide the three structures missing in the above chemical equation.

Experimental

Preparation of Grignard Reagent: Phenylmagnesium Bromide

Dry the following pieces of equipment a day before doing the experiment: a 10-mL round bottom flask, two 5-mL conical vials, a 25-mL Erlenmeyer flask, a Claisen head, spin vane, and a Pasteur pipette for use in dispensing ether. If, after drying as described, signs of water are still visible, dry the equipment in an oven. Prepare a drying tube with anhydrous calcium chloride.

First, obtain 0.075 g of *shiny* magnesium turnings, and place them into the *dry* round-bottom flask. Place a large *dry* spin vane or a magnetic stirring bar into the flask. Assemble the remainder of the apparatus as shown in class. Seal off the open end of the Claisen head with a rubber septum. *Transfer about 20 mL of anhydrous diethyl ether into a dry 25-mL Erlenmeyer flask, and stopper the flask. (**From the Instructor or Teaching Assistant**). During the experiment, remove the ether from the flask with a dry pipet*

Place 0.350 mL of bromobenzene (MW = 157.0) into a preweighed 5 mL conical vial, and determine the weight of the material transferred. Add 2.0 mL of anhydrous ether to the vial. After the bromobenzene dissolves, withdraw about 1.0 mL of this solution into 3-mL syringe and cap the vial. Inject the bromobenzene solution to the magnesium in the round-bottom flask. **You will need to save the remainder of the bromobenzene/ ether solution for later use.** Position the apparatus just above the hot plate. **DO NOT TURN ON THE HEAT!!** Stir the mixture gently to avoid throwing the magnesium onto the side of the flask. You should begin to notice the evolution of bubbles from the metal surface that signals that the reaction is starting.

When the reaction has started, you should observe the formation of a cloudy solution that could be any of a variety of colors. Remove more of the bromobenzene/ ether solution from the storage vial with the syringe, and add the solution slowly. Refill the syringe as necessary until all the solution has been added to the reaction flask . **Consult the instructor if no bubbles or color change has occurred.** As the reaction proceeds, you should observe the gradual disintegration of the magnesium metal. When all the bromobenzene has been added, place 1.0 mL of anhydrous ether in the vial that originally contained the bromobenzene solution, draw it into the syringe, and add the ether to the reaction mixture. Add more anhydrous ether (**check with instructor**) to replace any that is lost during the reflux period. After a period of 30 minutes from the beginning of the addition of bromobenzene, most or all of the magnesium should have reacted. Cool the mixture to room temperature.

Ketone Chemistry

During The Formation of Grignard

Prepare a solution of 0.55 g benzophenone in 1.5 mL of anhydrous ether in a 5-mL conical vial. Cap the vial until the reflux period is over.

Addition of Benzophenone

Once the Grignard reagent is cooled to room temperature, draw some of the benzophenone solution into the syringe and add it as rapidly (but not all at once) as possible to the stirred Grignard reagent. Add the remainder of the benzophenone solution with the syringe. Once the addition has been completed, cool the mixture to room temperature. *What Happened?* When stirring is no longer effective, remove the syringe and septum, and stir the mixture with a spatula. Rinse the vial that contained the benzophenone solution with about 0.5mL of anhydrous ether, and add it to the mixture. Remove the reaction flask from the apparatus, and cap it. Occasionally stir the contents of this flask. Recap the flask when it is standing to avoid contact with water vapor. The solid product should be fully formed after about 15 minutes.

To the reaction mixture add 3.0 mL of 6M hydrochloric acid (dropwise at first). Any unreacted magnesium will react with the acid. Use a spatula to break up the solid while adding the HCl. Because the neutralization procedure evolves heat, some ether will be lost due to evaporation. WHY? Add enough additional ether to maintain at least 3-5 mL volume in the upper organic phase. Eventually there will be two distinct layers: **Which layer will contain your product and why?** Make sure you have two distinct liquid layers, before separating the layers. More ether or HCl may be added if necessary to dissolve any remaining solid.

Transfer the organic phase (top or bottom layer?) to a small vial or 25-mL Erlenmeyer flask, leaving the stirring bar and aqueous phase behind. Add 2.5mL ether to the separated aqueous layer and shake to extract any remaining alcohol. Remove the ether and add this to the first ether extraction. Repeat the ether (2.5 mL) extraction once more. Discard the aqueous layer. Dry the organic layer (ether solution) with granular anhydrous sodium sulfate.

Decant the dried organic solution into a 10-mL Erlenmeyer flask, and rinse the drying agent with more diethyl ether. Evaporate the solvent in a hood by carefully heating the solution on a hot plate. After removal of the solvent, an oily solid should be left. This crude mixture contains the desired product and a by-product. Most of the by-product can be removed by adding 1.5mL of petroleum ether. *Petroleum ether is a mixture of hydrocarbons that easily dissolves the by-product and leaves behind the alcohol.* Do not confuse this solvent with diethyl ether ("ether"). Heat the mixture slightly, stir it, and cool it to room temperature. Collect the product by vacuum filtration on the Hirsh funnel and rinse it with small portions of petroleum ether. Air-dry the solid, weigh it, and calculate the percent yield of the crude product. Determine its melting point, and obtain an IR and NMR spectra.

Crystallize this product using *hot* isopropyl alcohol in an Erlenmeyer flask with a hot plate as the heating source. Be sure to add the hot alcohol in small portions to the crude product. Add the hot solvent until the solid just dissolves. Then allow the flask to cool slowly. When cooled, place the flask in an ice bath to complete the crystallization. Collect the solid on a small Hirsh funnel, and wash it with a small amount of *cold* isopropyl alcohol. Set the crystals aside to air-dry. Report the melting point of the purified product (literature value, 162°) and recovered yield in grams. Perform the assigned spectral analysis. Submit the sample to the instructor in a properly labeled vial.

Aldehyde Chemistry

During The Formation of Grignard

Transfer 2 mL anhydrous diethyl ether and 0.608 mL benzaldehyde in a 5-mL conical vial and shake the mixture.

Addition of Benzaldehyde

To the cool Grignard reagent add the aldehyde mixture dropwise over a period of 5 minutes. Rinse the vial that contained the aldehyde mixture with about 0.5mL of anhydrous ether, and add it to the mixture. After all of the mixture is added continue stirring for an additional 10 minutes (**consult your instructor**) and then disassemble the apparatus. To the mixture add dilute HCl solution (**prepared from 2 mL concentrated HCl and 20 mL of distilled water**) dropwise until the pH is neutral. What pH?

Transfer the organic phase (top or bottom layer?) to a small vial or 25-mL Erlenmeyer flask, leaving the stirring bar and aqueous phase behind. Add 2.5mL ether to the separated aqueous layer and shake to extract any remaining alcohol. Remove the ether and add this to the first ether extraction. Repeat the ether (2.5 mL) extraction once more. Discard the aqueous layer. Dry the organic layer (ether solution) with potassium carbonate for ten minutes or until the potassium carbonate moves freely.

Filter or decant the dried organic solution into a 10-mL Erlenmeyer flask, and rinse the drying agent with more diethyl ether. Concentrate (**in the HOOD**) the solution on medium heat until it is a syrup like texture. Remove from heat, and allow to cool to room temperature, once cooled place in an ice bath. **Why?** Collect the product and perform all necessary analysis. Submit your product with your conclusion.

Computational Chemistry (Spartan 2008 Molecular Model Program)

1.   Construct a model of the intermediate(s) and the product.

2.   Perform energy calculations, IR, and NMR.

1.   Pavia, D.L., Lampman, G.M., Kriz, G.S. and Engel, R.G., Introduction to Organic Laboratory Techniques, 3rd Ed., Saunders College Publishing, 1999, p. 292.

2.   Mohrig, J., Hammond, C., Morrill, T. and Neckers, D., Experimental Organic Chemistry (Macroscale and Microscale), Freeman Company, 1998, p.142-148.

3. Compare the energies between the possible intermediates.

4. Determine the percent difference of the calculated and experimental IR.

Waste Disposal

Collect all organic waste in a beaker during the experiment and dispose the combined waste at the end of the period into the **organic waste beaker in the HOOD**. All aqueous waste can be washed down the drain with plenty of water.

Writeup

Follow the directions in the syllabus.

Experiment 3
Grignard Reaction: Synthesis of an Alcohol

Name: _____

Prelab Exercise : Provide the structures missing in the chemical equations for these reactions.

Name: _____

Answer the following questions:

1. One reason why it is important to avoid side reactions in an organic reaction is that they lower the yield of the desired product. What is another important reason? What aspects of the experimental procedure were designed to minimize side reactions in this experiment?

2. The pink color during the Grignard reaction is due to the triphenyl cation, which is in equilibrium with the product, the magnesium salt of triphenylmethanol. The equilibrium reaction is shown below. Cations are not usually stable enough to be observed. Explain why the triphenylmethyl cation is observed, using chemical structures.

3.　Propose a different synthetic method for triphenylmethanol starting with benzene.

Synthesis of Benzocaine

Purpose

Benzocaine is a local anesthetic, and it is a product of an esterification reaction. In this experiment, you will prepare benzocaine from the reaction of p-aminobenzoic acid with ethanol and analyze it using IR,[1] HNMR and melting point.

Chemical Equation

$$CH_3CH_2OH / H^+$$

?

Prelab Exercise : Give the chemical structure and the IUPAC name for benzocaine.

Experimental

Place 0.120 g of p-aminobenzoic acid and 1.20 mL of absolute ethanol in a 5-mL conical vial. Add a magnetic stir vane, and stir the mixture until the solid dissolves completely. While stirring, add 0.10 mL concentrated sulfuric acid dropwise. What happened? Attach an air-condenser, and heat

1. Pavia, D.L., Lampman, G>M>, Kriz, G.S., and Engel, R.G., Introduction to Organic Laboratory Techniques, Saunders College Publishing, 1999, p. 350.

the mixture at a gentle boil for 45-75 minutes with a sand bath, while continuing to stir. What do you observe at the end of this period?

At the completion of heating, remove the apparatus from the sand bath and allow the reaction mixture to cool to room temperature. Transfer the contents of the vial to a small beaker containing 3.0 mL of water. Add (about 3 mL) of a 10% sodium carbonate solution dropwise to neutralize the mixture. What pH? Stir the contents of the beaker with a stirring rod. After each addition of the sodium carbonate solution, --------- occurs. What do you observe as the pH increases. Check the pH of the solution and add further portions of sodium carbonate until the pH is about 8. Collect the product by vacuum filtration using a Hirsh funnel.

Use three 1 mL portions of water to aid in the transfer and to wash the product in the funnel. Be sure that the solid is rinsed thoroughly with water. After the product has dried overnight, weigh it, calculate the percentage yield, and determine its melting point. Obtain IR and NMR sprectra. Submit the sample in a labeled vial with your report.

Although the product should be fairly pure, it may be recrystallized by the mixed solvent method using methanol and water. Place the product in a Craig tube; add several drops of methanol; and, while heating the Craig tube in a sand bath and stirring the stirring the mixture with a microspatula, add methanol dropwise until all the solid dissolves. Add two to three additional drops of methanol, and then add hot water dropwise until the mixture turns cloudy or a white precipitate forms. Add methanol again until the solid dissolves completely. Insert the inner plug of the Craig tube, and allow the solution to cool slowly to room temperature. Complete the recrystallization by cooling the mixture in an ice bath, and collect the crystals by centrifugation. Weigh the purified benzocaine, and determine its melting point.

Computational Chemistry (Spartan 2008 Molecular Model Program)

1. Construct a model of the intermediate(s) and the product.

2. Perform energy calculations, IR, and NMR.

3. Compare the energies between the possible intermediates.

4. Determine the percent difference of the calculated and experimental IR.

Waste Disposal

Collect the waste in a beaker during the experiment and dispose of it in the organic waste beaker in the HOOD.

Writeup

Follow the directions in the syllabus.

Experiment 4
Synthesis of Benzocaine

Name: _____

Prelab Exercise : Give the chemical structure and the IUPAC name for benzocaine.

Name: _____

Answer the following questions:

1. Give the structure of the precipitate that forms after the sulfuric acid has been added?

2. When 10% sodium carbonate solution is added, a gas evolves. What is the gas? Show a balanced chemical equation for this reaction.

3. Explain why benzocaine precipitates during the neutralization.

Aldol Condensation Reactions

Purpose

Condensation reactions are among the most important enolate reactions of carbonyl compounds. This experiment deals with the Aldol condensation reaction where two molecules of aldehyde or ketone (with α-hydrogen) combine to form β-hydroxyaldehyde or ketone which may go on to from α-β-unsaturated aldehyde or ketone. You will be assigned to prepare an aldol-product from **acetophenone** or **acetone**. At the end of the experiment, confirm the identity of the product using spectroscopic methods such as, melting point, IR, and ¹HNMR.

Chemical Equations

Reaction A:

$$1.\ ^-OH$$

$$2.\ H_3CO-\!\!\!\!\bigcirc\!\!\!\!-CHO$$

$$3.\ H_2O$$

$$\xrightarrow{\quad}\ ?\qquad \xrightarrow{\ ^-OH\ }\ ?$$

1.   Gilbert, J.C., and Martin, S.F., <u>Experimental Organic Chemistry, 3rd Ed</u>. Harcourt College Publishers, 2002, p. 570.

Reaction B:

Prelab Exercise : Give the missing chemical structures for the reactions above?

Experimental: Reaction A

Place 1.0 mL of p-anisaldehyde and 1.0 mL of acetophenone in a 10-mL Erlenmeyer flask and add 3.0mL of 95% ethanol. Shake the flask gently to dissolve the reactants.

Prepare a 50% (by mass) sodium hydroxide solution by dissolving 1.0 g sodium hydroxide in 1 mL water in a test tube. The solution may be heated gently to hasten dissolution, but be sure to cool the solution to room temperature before proceeding.

Using a Pasteur pipet, transfer 5 drops of the 50% sodium hydroxide solution into the ethanol solution of the carbonyl compounds, shake the mixture for a minute or two until a homogenous solution results, and allow to stand with occasional shaking at room temperature for 15 minutes. Cool the reaction mixture in an ice water bath. If crystals do not form, scratch the liquid-air interface to induce crystallization. Collect the product by vacuum filtration, wash the product with 1-2 mL of cold 95% ethanol, and air-dry the crystals. Recrystallize the crude product from methanol. Weigh the product and calculate the percent yield, determine its melting point. Obtain IR, ^{2}HNMR, and M.P. of your product. Submit the sample in a labeled vial to the instructor.

Experimental: Reaction B

Synthesis of Dibenzalacetone

In a 10-mL Erlenmeyer flask, place 2 mL of 3 M sodium hydroxide solution. To this add 1.6 mL of 95% ethanol and 0.212 g of benzaldehyde. Then add 0.058 g of acetone to the reaction mixture using density to determine the required volume of acetone in milliliters. Cap the flask immediately, and shake the mixture vigorously. **What is happening?** Continue to shake the flask from time to time for the next thirty minutes. If the product fails to crystallize, open the flask and scratch the inside with a glass rod. Remove the liquid from the flask using a Pasteur pipette

---

2.   Williamson, K.L., Macroscale and Microscale Organic Experiments, 3rd Ed., Houghton Mifflin Company, 1999, p. 441.

by squeezing the bulb of the pipette, pressing the tip against the bottom of the flask, and bringing the liquid into the pipette, leaving the crystals behind in the flask. Add 3 mL of water, cap, and shake the flask vigorously. Remove the wash liquid as before, and wash the crystals twice move with 3 mL portions of water.

After the final washing, add 3 mL water to the flask, and collect the crystals on a Hirsch funnel using vacuum filtration. Squeeze the product between sheets of filter paper to dry it, and then recrystallize the crude product from a 70:30 ethanol-water mixture. Remove the flask from the hot sand bath, and allow it to cool slowly to room temperature. Should the product separate as an oil, obtain a seed crystal from a classmate, heat the solution to dissolve the oil, and add the seed crystal as the solution cools. If it continues to oil out, add a small amount of ethanol. Collect the product on a Hirsch funnel by vacuum fitration and wash the crystals once with 1 mL of ice-cold 70% ethanol. Dry the product under vacuum by attaching the flask to an aspirator. Determine the weight of the desired product, IR, NMR, and melting point. Also calculate the percentage yield of the product. Submit sample to the instructor.

Computational Chemistry (Spartan 2008 Molecular Model Program)

1. Construct a model of the intermediate(s) and the product.

2. Perform energy calculations, IR, and NMR.

3. Compare the energies between the possible intermediates.

4. Determine the percent difference of the calculated and experimental IR.

Waste Disposal

All organic waste (filtrates, etc...) go into the organic waste container in the HOOD.

Writeup

Follow directions in the syllabus.

Experiment 5
Aldol Condensation Reactions

Name: _____

Prelab Exercise : Give the missing structures for the reactions on page 21.

Name: _____

Answer the following questions:

1)   Propose a synthesis of cinnamaldehyde using a crossed aldol condensation.

2)   Write structures for the various aldol condensation products expected from the aldol self-condensation of 2-butanone.

3)   Identify the nucleophile and electrophile involved in the rate-determining step of **Reaction A or Reaction B.**

The Diels-Alder
Cycloaddition Reaction

Purpose

The Diels-Alder reaction is an extremely useful synthetic reaction since it is one of the best ways to make a six-membered ring with diverse functionality and controlled stereochemistry. In this experiment, you will make the aldol-product first, and then react it with dimethyl acetylenedicarboxylate to give the final product. Using melting point, IR and 1HNMR determine the identity of the product.

Chemical Equation

1.   Williamson, K.L., <u>Macroscale and Microscale Organic Experiments, 3<u>rd</u> Ed.</u>, Houghton Mifflin Company, 1999, p. 600-609.

Prelab Exercise : Write the IUPAC names and the structural formulas for the aldol-product and the Diels-Alder product.

Experimental

Part 1   Synthesis of the Aldol-Product

WARNING : Triton B is harmful and corrosive.

Into a clean and dried 10 x 100 mm reaction tube place 84 mg of pure benzil, 0.070 mL of 1,3-diphenylacetone, and 0.8 mL of triethylene glycol. Clamp the test tube and place it in a hot sand bath, and heat the solution until the benzyl is dissolved. Remove the tube from the heat, and then using a 1 mL syringe, add to the solution 0.4 mL of a 40% solution of benzyltrimethylammonium hydroxide in methanol (Triton B) when the temperature of the solution reaches exactly 100°C. Stir once to mix. Crystallization usually starts in 20 to 30 seconds. Let the mixture cool to near room temperature, and then cool it in an ice bath. Add 1.0 mL of methanol, continue to cool in ice bath, and collect the product by vacuum filtration.

If the crystals are large enough, collection can be done by inserting a Pasteur pipette into the tube and removing the solvent between the tip of the pipette and the bottom of the tube. In any case, wash the crystals with cold methanol until the washings are purple-pink, not brown. If either the crystals are not well formed or the melting point is low, place the material in a reaction tube, add 1.2 mL of triethylene glycol, and raise the temperature to 220°C to bring the solid into solution. Let it stand for crystallization.

Part 2   Cycloaddition Reaction

WARNING :   Work in a HOOD because of toxic fumes that will be generated in this part of the experiment.

Measure into a reaction tube 50 mg of the product from the above reaction, 0.4 mL of 1,2-dichlorobenzene, and 27.5 mg or (0.25 mL, if it is a liquid) of dimethyl acetylenedicarboxylate. Clamp the tube over a hot sand bath, insert a thermometer, and raise the temperature of the mixture to 180-185°C. Boil gently until there is no further color change, and let the rim of the condensate rise just enough to wash the walls of the tube. A 10-min. boiling period should be sufficient. Cool the tube to 100°C, slowly stir in 0.6 mL of 95% ethanol, and let crystallization proceed. After the mixture has cooled to near-room temperature, cool it on ice. Collect the product, either by vacuum filtration(wash the crystals with cold methanol) or centrifugation using The Craig tube.

Computational Chemistry (Spartan 2008 Molecular Model Program)

1.   Construct a model of the intermediate(s) and the product.

2.   Perform energy calculations, IR, and NMR.

3. Compare the energies between the possible intermediates.

4. Determine the percent difference of the calculated and experimental IR.

Waste Disposal

Since the filtrate and washings from **Part A** contain Triton B, they should be placed in the hazardous waste container, along with the crystallization solvent. The filtrate from **Part B** contains 1,2-dichlorobenzene, it should be placed in the halogenated organic solvents container in the HOOD.

Writeup

Follow the directions in the syllabus.

Experiment 6
The Diels-Alder Cycloaddition Reaction

Name: _____

Prelab Exercise : Write the IUPAC names and the structural formulas for the aldol-product and the Diels-Alder product.

Name: ————————————————————————————————————

Answer the following questions:

1. The formation of carbon monoxide in this reaction can be thought of as the driving force for this reaction. How else can stability be used to explain the ease of the reaction?

2. If a Diels-Alder reaction was conducted using 38.4g (0.1 mol) of tetraphenylcyclopentdienone, what volume of CO, measured at STP (0° C and 1 atm) would be produced?

Polymers and Polymerization

Purpose

The polymers you are going to prepare represent some of the important commercial plastics. There are two types of reaction for the formation of polymers, addition (polystyrene) and condensation (linear polyester, cross-linked polyester, nylon). In this experiment, you will prepare three examples of a condensation polymer. At the end of the experiment you will determine the weight and physical properties of these polymers.

Chemical Equation for Polyesters

phthalic anhydride   ethylene glycol   ?

phthalic anhydride   glycerol   ?

Chemical Equation for Nylon

Adipoyl   chloride   Hexamethylenediamine

Prelab Exercise : Give the structural formulas of the three polymers.

Experimental

Polyesters

Place 2 g of phthalic anhydride and 0.1 g of sodium acetate in each of two test tubes. To one tube add 0.8 mL of ethylene glycol, and to the other add 0.8 mL glycerol. Stir the mixture before heating. Clamp both tubes so that they can be heated simultaneously with a flame. Heat the tubes gently until the solutions appear to boil, then continue to heat for 5 minutes. Pour the hot solutions onto separate pieces of aluminum foil and allow them to cool to room temperature. Carefully peel the polymers off the foil. Weigh the polymers and compare their properties.

Polyamide (Nylon)

Pour 10 mL of a 5% aqueous solution of hexamethylenediamine (1,6-hexanediamine) into a 50-mL beaker. Add 10 drops of 20% (6M) sodium hydroxide solution. To this solution, carefully add 10 mL of a 5% solution of adipoyl chloride in cyclohexane down the wall of a slightly tilted beaker. Two layers will form and there will be an immediate formation of a polymer film at the liquid-liquid interface. Using tweezers grab the white mass at the interface and slowly raise the tweezers so that Nylon forms continuously, producing a rope that can be drawn out. Use a test tube to wind the rope slowly as long as it continues to form. If the rope breaks, restart the process of winding. Wash the polymer with plenty of water and then dry it with paper towel. Weigh the dried Nylon and either discard it properly or keep it as a souvenir.

---

1.   Pavia, Lampman, Kriz and Engel, Introduction to Organic Laboratory Techniques, A Microscale Approach, 3rd Ed. Saunders College Publishing 1999, p. 395.

Waste Disposal

Place the two reaction test tubes into the box designated for broken or cracked glass. The solution from the nylon experiment goes into the organic waste beaker in the HOOD. You are free to take the polyesters and nylon home with you or discard them in the waste basket.

Writeup

Follow the directions in the syllabus

Experiment 7
Polymers and Polymerization

Name: _____

Prelab Exercise : Give the structural formulas of the three polymers.

Reduction of Vanillin using Sodium Borohydride

Purpose

Reduction of carbonyl compounds using metal hydrides ($LiAlH_4$, $NaBH_4$) as reducing agents are common and important in most organic laboratories. In this experiment, you will prepare vanillyl alcohol. At the end of the experiment, you will perform the following analyses (IR, MP, TLC and ^{1}HNMR) to confirm the identity of the reaction product.

Chemical Equation

1. Lehman, J.W., Multiscale Operational Organic Chemistry, A Problem-Solving Approach to the Laboratory Course, Prentice Hall, 2002, p. 223

Prelab Exercise:

1. Identify and name the functional groups in vanillin.

2. What is the IUPAC name for vanillin?

3. Predict the product and give a complete balanced equation of the reaction

Experimental

Weigh and place 0.76 g of vanillin in a 25 mL Erlenmeyer flask. Add 5.5 mL of 1M sodium hydroxide solution and a spin vane. Cool the flask in an ice bath to 10-15 °C. While stirring, add 0.20 g of sodium borohydride in portions over a period of about 2-3 minutes. Remove the flask from the ice bath and allow it to stand at room temperature for 20 minutes.

After 20 minutes, place the flask in an ice bath and add 1M hydrochloric acid slowly while stirring until the mixture is weakly acidic. What pH? Use a stirring rod and gently scratch the bottom of the flask. Why? Cool the mixture for 30 minutes and collect the product by vacuum filtration using a Hirsch funnel. Wash the product with cold distilled water (2 x 2mL) and allow it to air dry on the funnel for 20-30 minutes.

Recrystallize the crude product from a minimum amount of ethyl acetate. Allow the solution to cool to room temperature and then cool further in an ice bath. Collect the desired product by vacuum filtration. Perform all the necessary analyses and submit your product in a vial to your instructor.

Computational Chemistry (Spartan 2008 Molecular Model Program)

1. Construct a model of the intermediate(s) and the product.

2. Perform energy calculations, IR, and NMR.

3. Compare the energies between the possible intermediates.

4. Determine the percent difference of the calculated and experimental IR.

Waste Disposal

To the first filtrate, add solid sodium bicarbonate while stirring until foaming ceases. Flush the mixture down the drain with plenty of water.

The filtrate from the recrystallization must be disposed of in the **waste organic container in the HOOD**.

Writeup

Follow the direction in your syllabus.

Name: ———————————————————————————————————————

Answer the following questions:

1. Give the structure of the intermediate product that was formed after the addition of sodium borohydride.

2. What is the purpose of hydrochloric acid in this reaction?

Name: _____

Prelab Exercise:

1. Identify and name the functional groups in vanillin.

2. What is the IUPAC name for vanillin?

3. Predict the product and give a complete balanced equation of the reaction

Wittig Reaction

Purpose

Wittig reaction is one of many methods used in the preparation of alkenes. In this reaction, a carbonyl compound (an aldehyde or ketone) is treated with a Wittig reagent to produce an alkene. In this experiment you will synthesize an alkene, and then confirm its identity by performing the following analyses: m.p., IR, TLC and ^{1}HNMR.

Chemical Equation A

1. Williamson, K.L., Macroscale and <u>Microscale Organic Experiments, 3rd Ed.</u>, Houghton Mifflin Company, 1999, p. 464.

Chemical Equation B

Prelab Exercise:

1. Complete the above chemical equations for the reaction.

2. Is the product a conjugated system or not? Explain.

3. Identify and name the Wittig reagent in this reaction.

4. Give the IUPAC name for the product in this reaction.

Experimental A

To a dry 25 mL Erlenmeyer flask using a syringe add 3 mL of anhydrous methanol, 0.60 g of benzyltriphenylphosphonium chloride, 0.20 g of cinnamaldehyde (freshly distilled), and a spin vane. With rapid stirring, add 0.40 mL or 0.10 g of sodium methoxide. Continue to stir for 30 minutes at room temperature. Collect the crude product by suction filtration on a Hirsch funnel. Rinse the flask with 1 mL of cold methanol and transfer the mixture into the funnel. Wash the crude product with two 2 mL portions of cold distilled water. Allow the crude product to air dry for about 20-30 minutes.

Recrystallize the crude product from a minimum amount of methanol. After cooling to room temperature, cool the flask in an ice bath and then collect the product on the Hirsch funnel. Rinse the product with 2 ml of cold methanol and then allow to air dry for twenty minutes. Perform the required analyses to identify your product.

Experimental B

Place 1.0 mL of anhydrous methanol, 0.40 mL of 25 wt % sodium methoxide/methanol solution, and 0.43 mL of trimethyl phosphonoacetate in a 5 mL vial containing a spin vane. Close the vial with a screw cap and septum immediately. Insert a syringe needle through the septum and stir.

---

2.   Bottin-Strzalko, T. *Tetrahedron* **1973**, 29, 4199-4204.

3.   Crandall, J.K.; Mayer, C.F. **J. Organic Chemistry**. 1970, 35, 3049-3053

Prepare a solution of 0.20 mL of p-anisaldehyde and 0.50 mL of anhydrous methanol in a dry test tube or vial. Add (using syringe) this solution slowly to the reaction mixture over a period of 10 minutes. Continue to stir the reaction mixture at room temperature for 1 hour. At the end of the reaction period, open the vial and add 2.0 mL of distilled water, close the vial and shake it.

Collect the crude product by vacuum filtration on a Hirsch funnel. Rinse the vial with 1 mL of distilled water and add to the Hirsch funnel and then allow the crude product to air dry for 20-30 minutes under vacuum.

Purify the product by recrystallization from 95% ethanol in a 10 mL Erlenmeyer flask. When the crystals have dissolved completely, add distilled water dropwise to the hot solution until cloudiness occurs, then add 95% ethanol dropwise until the solution clears.

Allow the solution to cool to room temperature before placing it in an ice bath. Collect the desired product by vacuum filtration on a Hirsch funnel. Wash the product with 1 mL of cold 95% ethanol and then allow it to air dry before performing the required analyses.

Computational Chemistry (Spartan 2008 Molecular Model Program)

1. Construct a model of the intermediate(s) and the product.

2. Perform energy calculations, IR, and NMR.

3. Compare the energies between the possible intermediates.

4. Determine the percent difference of the calculated and experimental IR.

Waste Disposal

Collect all organic waste in a beaker during the experiment and dispose of the combined waste at the end of the period into the **waste organic container in the HOOD**.

Writeup

Follow the direction in your syllabus.

Experiment 9
Wittig Reaction

Name: —————————————————————————————

Prelab Exercise:

1. Complete the above chemical equations for the reaction.

2. Is the product a conjugated system or not? Explain.

3. Identify and name the Wittig reagent in this reaction.

4. Give the IUPAC name for the product in this reaction.

Name: ───

Answer the following questions:

1. Write chemical equations for the preparation of the following alkenes by Wittig reactions. Start with any carbonyl compound and Wittig reagent together with any other organic or inorganic reagents that you require.

a)

b)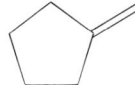

c)

2. Suggest a method for preparing benzyltriphenylphosphonium chloride via an S_N2 reaction.

3. Write the two resonance forms of Wittig reagents.

Electrophilic Aromatic Substitution: Chlorination of a Disubstituted Benzene

Purpose

The goal of this experiment is to determine the competitiveness of two activating groups on a disubstituted benzene. At the end of the experiment, you will perform the following analysis (IR, ^{1}HNMR and MP) to confirm the identity of the reaction product.

Chemical Equation

Prelab Exercise : Which of two possible products result from the chlorination of 4-bromoacetanilide?

1.   Ault, A. and Kraig R., J. Chem. Edu. 1966, 43, 213.

Experimental

WARNING : **Concentrated Hydrochloric Acid is very corrosive! Wear gloves when handling this chemical to avoid burns. Dispense this chemical in the hood to avoid any inhalation. Should any spills occur while dispensing this chemical, wash the affected area under cold running water. Perform all work in the HOOD.**

Place 2.4 ml of concentrated hydrochloric acid and 2.8 ml of glacial acetic acid in a 25 ml Erlenmeyer flask containing a spin vane. While this mixture is stirring, add 1.07 g of 4-bromoacetanilide. Heat this mixture in a sand bath until all solid is dissolved. Allow the mixture to cool to room temperature and then place it in an ice bath until temperature reaches 0 °C. To the cold solution, gradually add a solution of 0.278 g of sodium chlorate dissolved in 0.7 ml of distilled water.

Allow the reaction mixture to stir for one hour at room temperature. Collect the product by vacuum filtration. Wash the crude product with distilled water (2 x 5 mL) and then allow it to dry on the funnel for about 30 min or more. Determine its melting point, percent yield, and IR.

Weigh and place 1.24 g of the above product into a 10-mL round-bottom flask. To the solid, add 2 ml of 95% ethanol and 1.3 ml of concentrated hydrochloric acid. Attach a reflux condenser or an air condenser and heat in a sand bath for 30-45 minutes. Transfer the mixture into a 25 ml Erlenmeyer flask and add 8 ml of HOT distilled water with stirring. Allow stirring to occur for 5-10 minutes. Pour the mixture into a 100 ml beaker containing 15 g of ice and add 1.2 ml of 50% sodium hydroxide solution. Collect the final product by vacuum filtration on a Hirsh funnel. Rinse the product with 5 ml of cold distilled water 3 times. Allow rinsed product to dry overnight. Perform the required analysis to identify the product.

Computational Chemistry (Spartan 2008 Molecular Model Program)

1. Construct a model of the intermediate(s) and the product.
2. Perform energy calculations, IR, and NMR.
3. Compare the energies between the possible intermediates.
4. Determine the percent difference of the calculated and experimental IR.

Waste Disposal

Collect all organic waste in a beaker during the experiment and dispose of the combined waste at the end of the period into the **organic waste container inside the HOOD.**

Write-up

Follow the directions in the syllabus.

2. Ault, A. Techniques and Experiments for Organic Chemistry, 6th ed., Waveland Press: Prospect Heights, II, 1998; pp. 615-622.

3. Schoffstall, A.M., Gaddis, B.A., Druelinger, M.L. Microscale and Miniscale Organic Chemistry Laboratory Experiments. McGraw Hill: Boston, MA 2000, Chapter 22.

Experiment 10
Chlorination of a Disubstituted Benzene

Name: _____

Prelab Exercise : Which of two possible products result from the chlorination of 4-bromoacetanilide?

Further your understanding of the chemistry in this lab by answering the following questions:

Name: _____

1. Propose a synthesis for 4-bromoacetanilide from benzene.

Synthesis of Phenacetin

Important: This is a nucleophilic acyl substitution reaction combined with Williamson ether synthesis. Three to four days experiment.

Purpose

This is a two part experiment. The first part deals with the nucleophilic acyl substitution reaction preparing Tylenol. The Tylenol then acts as an intermediate to react with an alkyl halide via a S_N2 mechanism to produce the ether.

Chemical Equation:

1.   Lehman, John W. Operational Organic Chemistry: A Laboratory Course, 2nd ed., Allyn and Bacon, Inc., 1988, p. 253.

Prelab Exercise : Provide the two missing structures in the above chemical equation.

Experimental

WARNING : Concentrated Hydrochloric Acid is very corrosive! Wear gloves when handling this chemical to avoid burns. Dispense this chemical in the hood to avoid any inhalation. Should any spills occur while dispensing this chemical, wash the affected area under cold running water.

Weigh and place 1.1 g of p-Aminophenol into a 25 ml Erlenmeyer flask with a spin vane. Add 10 ml of distilled water and 0.9 ml of concentrated hydrochloric acid with stirring until all solid is dissolved. After solid has dissolved, add 1.1 g of acetic anhydride to the mixture with stirring. To the homogeneous mixture, add the sodium acetate solution (this solution is prepared by mixing 1.0 g of anhydrous sodium acetate in 6 ml of distilled water). Allow this mixture to stir for 30-45 minutes at room temperature. Collect the product via vacuum filtration in a Hirsh funnel. Wash the solid product with 5 ml of COLD distilled water 3 times and allow it to dry overnight. Determine the melting point, percent yield, and IR.

Weigh and place 0.375 g of the product into a 10 ml round bottom flask with a spin vane.

Add 2.5 ml of methanol and 0.1575 ml of 50% NaOH into the flask with stirring until the solid is completely dissolved. Attach a reflux condenser or air condenser and add 0.375 ml of ethyl bromide through (down) the condenser. Heat the reaction mixture in a sand bath for 2 hours. After reflux, remove heat and add 5.0 ml of HOT distilled water down the condenser. Cool the flask down to room temperature for 30 minutes. Collect the product via vacuum filtration on a Hirsh funnel. Wash the solid product with 5 ml of COLD distilled water 3 times and dry it overnight. Perform the required analysis on the dried product.

Computational Chemistry (Spartan 2008 Molecular Model Program)

1. Construct a model of the intermediate(s) and the product.

2. Perform energy calculations, IR, and NMR.

3. Compare the energies between the possible intermediates.

4. Determine the percent difference of the calculated and experimental IR.

Waste Disposal

Collect all organic waste in a beaker during the experiment and dispose the combined waste at the end of the period into the **organic waste container inside the HOOD.**

Write-up

Follow the directions given in the syllabus.

Experiment 11
Synthesis of Phenacetin

Name: _____

Prelab Exercise : Provide the two missing structures in the above chemical equation.

Name: _____

Answer the following questions:

1. Write structures for some by-products that might form during the synthesis of phenacetin, and give equations and mechanisms for their formation.

2.   Starting with benzene, outline a synthesis for the formation of the compound below:

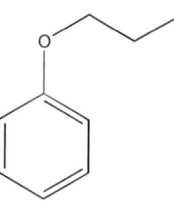

Chemistry of Vanillin

Purpose

A primary focus in this project is the chemical transformations of functional groups, and substitution of the aromatic ring. Reduction of the aldehyde group using a metal hydride, $NaBH_4$ will be the final step of each project. This is a two step project and the starting reagent is vanillin. This compound contains several functional groups and it's the key ingredient of most flavored compounds. At the end of each experiment, you will perform the following analyses (IR, MP, TLC and ^1HNMR) to confirm the identity of the reaction product(s).

1.   Addison Ault, <u>Techniques and Experiments for Organic Chemistry</u>, Sixth Edition, University Science Books, Sausalito, California, 1998, p. 485.

Chemical Equations

$? \xrightarrow{\text{NaBH}_4} ?$ Project B

$\uparrow$ $(CH_3CH_2O)_2O$

$\xrightarrow{\text{Br}_2/\text{CH}_3\text{COOH}} ? \xrightarrow{\text{NaBH}_4} ?$

Project A

$\downarrow$ HNO_3/CH_3COOH

$? \xrightarrow{\text{NaBH}_4} ?$ Project C

Prelab Exercise:

1. Identify and name the functional groups in vanillin.

2. What is the IUPAC name for vanillin?

3. Provide the two missing structures and their names in the above chemical equation.

Experimental

Project A

Place 1.01 g and 4 mL of glacial acetic acid in a 50 ml Erlenmeyer flask containing a spin vane. While stirring, add 4 mL of 2 M solution of bromine in glacial acetic acid (10.2 mL of bromine to 90 mL of glacial acetic acid) to the reaction flask. Stir for 5-10 min and then allow the reaction mixture to stand overnight at room temperature.

Collect the product by vacuum filtration, and wash with cold distilled water (3 X 10 mL). Recrystallize the crude from minimum amount of ethanol to obtain a pure product. *Perform all the necessary analyses.*

Project B

Weigh and place 1.01 g of vanillin in a 50 mL Erlenmeyer flask. Add 7.4 mL of 1 M potassium hydroxide solution and a spin vane. While stirring, add 0.7 mL of acetic anhydride in 15 mL of diethyl ether. Continue to stir for 20-30 min. What happened?

Make sure you have two distinct liquid layers before separating the layers. Transfer the organic layer into a clean Erlenmeyer flask; dry the solution with anhydrous sodium sulfate. Decant the dried organic solution into a clean dry 25-mL Erlenmeyer flask. Concentrate the solvent in a hood by carefully heating the solution on a hot plate. Allow the crude to cool to room temperature. What happened?

Recrystallize the crude product using minimum amount of 1:1 ethanol/water mixture. Collect the product by vacuum filtration and rinse it with the above mixture. Allow the product to air-dry for 20-30 min. *Perform all the necessary analyses.*

Project C

Place 1.01 g of vanillin and 13.5 mL of glacial acetic acid in a 50-mL Erlenmeyer flask containing a spin vane. Place the flask in an ice bath and stir for 10 min. To this stirring solution, add 0.5 mL of concentrated nitric acid dissolved in 4 mL of glacial acetic acid dropwise for a period of 2-3 min. What happened?

At the end of the addition, continue to stir the mixture for an additional 5 min, and then add 16 mL of cold distilled water. Stir the mixture for 5 min and then collect the product by vacuum filtration. Wash the product with water (3 X 5 mL), followed by methanol (3 x 5 mL). Collect the product and recrystallize from 20-30 mL of ethyl acetate. *Perform all the necessary analyses.*

Reduction Procedure

Weigh and place 0.76 g of your product in a 50 mL Erlenmeyer flask. Add 5.5 mL of 1M sodium hydroxide solution (**Add water instead for project B.**) and a spin vane. Cool the flask in an ice bath to 10-15 °C. While stirring, add 0.20 g of sodium borohydride in portions over a period of about 2-3 minutes. Remove the flask from the ice bath and allow it to stand at room temperature for 20 minutes.

After 20 minutes, place the flask in an ice bath and add 1M hydrochloric acid (**Not project B**) slowly while stirring until the mixture is weakly acidic. What pH? Use a stirring rod and gently scratch the bottom of the flask. Why? Cool the mixture for 30 minutes (**For Project B and C, place the mixture in the refrigerator for 2 hr or more**) and collect the product by vacuum filtration using a Hirsch funnel. Wash the product with cold distilled water (3 x 5 mL) and allow it to air dry on the funnel for 20-30 minutes.

Recrystallize the crude product from a minimum amount of ethyl acetate. Allow the solution to cool to room temperature and then cool further in an ice bath. Collect the desired product by vacuum filtration. Perform all the necessary analyses and submit your product in a vial to your instructor.

Computational Chemistry (Spartan 2008 Molecular Model Program)

1. Construct a model of the intermediate(s) and the product.

2. Perform energy calculations, IR, and NMR.

3. Compare the energies between the possible intermediates.

4. Determine the percent difference of the calculated and experimental IR.

Waste Disposal

Collect all organic waste in a beaker at your bench and dispose it in the **waste organic container in the HOOD at the end of the period**.

Writeup

Follow the direction in your syllabus.

---

2. Lehman, J.W., Multiscale Operational Organic Chemistry, A Problem-Solving Approach to the Laboratory Course, Prentice Hall, 2002, p. 223

3. Arrey, L.N., Investigative Experimental Organic Chemistry, Microscale Approach, 2006, pg 35.

Experiment 12
Chemistry of Vanillin

Name: _____

Prelab Exercise:

1. Identify and name the functional groups in vanillin.

2. What is the IUPAC name for vanillin?

3. Provide the two missing structures and their names in the above chemical equation.

Name: ————————————————————————————————————

Further your understanding of the chemistry in this lab by answering the following question:

Propose a complete synthetic method of your final product starting with benzene.

Chemistry of Bromobenzene

Important: This is an electrophilic/ nucleophilic aromatic substitution reaction.

Purpose

This is a two part experiment. The first part deals with electrophilic aromatic substitution using a nitrating agent. The nitro-compound then acts as an intermediate to react with a variety of nucleophiles via a S_N2 mechanism to produce the final product. Using melting point, IR and ^{1}HNMR determine the identity of the product.

1.   Addison Ault, <u>Techniques and Experiments for Organic Chemistry</u>, Sixth Edition, University Science Books, Sausalito, California, 1998, p. 469.

Chemical Equation:

Prelab Exercise : Provide the two missing structures in the above **chemical equation.**

Experimental

WARNING : Concentrated Sulfuric Acid and Nitric Acids are **very corrosive! Wear gloves when handling** these chemicals to avoid **burns. Dispense these chemicals in the hood to avoid any inhalation. Should any spills occur while dispensing these chemicals, wash the affected area under cold running water.**

Place 5 mL of concentrated sulfuric acid and 2 mL of concentrated nitric acid in a 25-mL Erlenmeyer flask containing a spin vane and heat the mixture to 85-90 °C. To the reaction flask, add 0.7 mL of bromobenzene dropwise for 2-3 min. Check the temperature of the reaction. What happened?

Remove the flask from the heating source and continue to stir. Allow the mixture to cool to room temperature, and then pour it over 30 g of ice in a 100-mL beaker. Stir the mixture until the product solidifies. Collect the product by vacuum filtration and wash it with cold distilled water (3 x 5 mL).

Recrystallize the crude product from minimum amount of 95 % ethanol. Rinse the product with cold 95 % ethanol (2 x 3 mL), allow it to air-dry for 10 min before *collecting and performing all the necessary analyses.*

Project A

Weigh and place 0.65 g of your product in a 25-mL Erlenmeyer flask containing a spin vane. To the flask, add 7 mL of ethanol. Gently heat and stir the mixture until the solid dissolves. To this solution, add 5 mL of concentrated ammonium hydroxide and allow the reaction to stand at room temperature for four days.

Collect the crude product and recrystallize it from minimum amount of a mixture of water and ethanol (1:3 ratio). Use vacuum filtration to collect the final product and wash it with water/ ethanol mixture (2 x 3 mL). Allow the product to dry and then *perform all the necessary analyses.*

Project B

Weigh 0.6 g of your product and place it into a 25-mL round-bottom flask containing a spin vane. Add 7 mL of ethanol, and then attach a water condenser to the flask. To the mixture add 0.86 g of 4-bromoaniline. Heat the mixture gently with stirring under reflux until all the solid has dissolved. Remove the flask from the heating source and allow the mixture to cool to room temperature. Collect the crude using vacuum filtration and wash it with cold ethanol (2 x 5 mL).

Recrystallize the product from minimum amount of ethanol. Allow the solution to cool to room temperature, and then place it in an ice bath for crystals to form. Collect the product by vacuum filtration and wash with cold ethanol (2 x 3 mL). Allow the product to air-dry, and then *perform all the necessary analyses.*

Project C

In a 50-mL round-bottom flask containing a spin vane, place 0.6 g of your product and then add 7 mL of ethanol. To the mixture add 0.5 g of aniline. Fit a water condenser to the flask and heat under reflux to dissolve the solid. Remove the heat and allow the reaction to cool to room temperature. Collect the crude using vacuum filtration and wash with cold ethanol (2 x 3 mL).

Purify the crude product by recrystallization from minimum amount of 95 % ethanol. Collect, and wash the product with cold ethanol (2 x 3 mL). Allow the product to air-dry for 20 min, and then *perform all necessary analyses.*

Project D

Weigh and place 0.5 g of your product into a 50-mL Erlenmeyer flask containing a spin vane. Add 7.5 mL of 95 % ethanol to the flask and heat almost to boiling. To the hot mixture, add a solution of 0.5 mL of 64 % hydrazine in 2.5 mL of 95 % ethanol. Allow the resulting mixture to cool to room temperature. Collect the crude product by vacuum filtration. Wash the crude with cold ethanol (3 x 3 mL).

Recrystallize the crude from minimum amount of ethyl acetate. Collect the purified product by vacuum filtration, wash with cold ethyl acetate (2 x 3 mL), air-dry for 20 min, and then *perform all the necessary analyses.*

Computational Chemistry (Spartan 2008 Molecular Model Program)

1.   Construct a model of the intermediate(s) and the product.

2.   Perform energy calculations, IR, and NMR.

3.   Compare the energies between the possible intermediates.

4.   Determine the percent difference of the calculated and experimental IR.

Waste Disposal

Collect all organic waste in a beaker during the experiment and dispose the combined waste at the end of the period into the **organic waste container inside the HOOD.**

Write-up

Follow the directions given in the syllabus.

Experiment 13
Chemistry of Bromobenzene

Name: _____

Prelab Exercise : Provide the two missing structures in the above chemical equation.

Name: _____

Answer the following questions:

1. Starting with benzene, outline a synthesis for the formation of the final compound that you synthesized.

2. Provide a detailed reaction mechanism for the Nucleophilic substitution part of the experiment.

Synthesis of an aromatic Ether

Purpose

The goal of this experiment is the determination of the product of this reaction. In this reaction, an aromatic alcohol is converted into a nucleophile which then reacts with an alkyl halide to yield an aromatic ether. This reaction is known as Williamson ether synthesis. At the end of the experiment, you will perform the following analysis (MP, IR, ^{1}HNMR, ChemDraw and Spartan calculations) to confirm the identity of the reaction product.

Chemical Equation

Prelab Exercise : Identify and name the missing compounds in the chemical equation above.

Experimental

WARNING: Add the reagents and initiate the reaction in the hood.

Measure and place 2.5 mL of methanol in a 10.0 mL round-bottomed flask containing a spin vane. Add 1.0 g of β-naphthol to the flask followed by 1.0 mL of 25% sodium hydroxide solution. To

---

the mixture, add 0.8 mL of ethyl iodide using a syringe without the needle. Attach an air condenser to the flask and heat it for 30-45 min. on your bench using a sand bath. Pour the reaction mixture into a beaker containing 5 ml of ice-cold water. What happened? Add 6 mL of diethyl ether, stir with a glass rod and then extract the organic phase and transfer to an Erlenmeyer flask. To the aqueous phase add 5 mL of diethyl ether and transfer it to the flask containing the first organic phase. Dry the combined organic phase with anhydrous sodium sulfate. Decant the dried-liquid into a 25 or 50-mL Erlenmeyer flask and then concentrate on a sand bath. What happened?

To the flask add 10 ml of 95% ethanol and heat the mixture to half its volume. Allow the mixture to cool to room temperature and then place it in an ice bath for 20 minutes. What happened? Collect the crystals by vacuum filtration using a Hirsch funnel (*For references relating to the use of Hirsch funnel, see Organic Chemistry Laboratory Techniques by L. Nyenty Arrey*). Wash the crystals with two 1-mL portions of cold ethanol. Allow the crystals to dry for 10-20 min and then weigh and calculate the percent yield. Perform the necessary analysis to identify your product

Computational Chemistry (Spartan 2008 Molecular Model Program)

1. Construct a model of the intermediate(s) and the product.

2. Perform energy calculations, IR, and NMR.

3. Compare the energies, and bond lengths of benzyne with those of benzene.

4. Determine the percent difference of the calculated and experimental IR.

Waste Disposal

Collect all organic waste in a beaker during the experiment and dispose of the combined waste at the end of the period into the **organic waste beaker in the HOOD**.

Writeup

Follow the directions in the syllabus.

Experiment 14
Synthesis of an aromatic Ether

Name: _____

Prelab Exercise : Identify and name the missing compounds in the chemical equation above.

Experiment 14

Further your understanding of the chemistry in this lab by answering the following questions:

Name: _____

1. Explain why phenols, including the β-naphthol, which is used in the current experiment, would be acidic and why it easily reacts with base. Chemical equations might be helpful.

2. Sodium hydroxide reacts with b-naphthol to form the sodium salt. Can sodium ethoxide, the sodium salt of ethanol be formed the same way? If not, what is an effective way to produce sodium ethoxide which can be used in organic reactions?

3.   What is meant by "seeding"? Explain the process.

Synthesis of Caprolactam

Important : This is a ring expansion reaction.

Purpose

This is a two part experiment. The first part deals with the formation of cyclohexanone oxime from cyclohexanone. The second part is conversion of cyclohexanone oxime to caprolactam via a Beckman Rearrangement process. Using melting point, IR and ^{1}HNMR determine the identity of the product. ChemDraw and Spartan calculations will be examined.

Chemical Equation:

$$\text{cyclohexanone} \xrightarrow{NH_2OH} \quad ? \quad \xrightarrow{H_2SO_4} \quad ? \quad \xrightarrow{NH_2OH} \quad ?$$

Prelab Exercise:

Provide the missing structures and their names in the above chemical equation.

---

1. Kun Qiao, Youquan Deng, Chiaki Yokoyama, Hikaru Sato and **Miki** Yamashina, Preparation of ε-Caprolactam via Beckmann Rearrangement of Cyclohexanone Oxime: A Mild and Recyclable Process, Chemistry Letters, 2004, vol. 33, No.

2. <http://people.clarkson.edu/~ochem/Spring01/CM244/caprolactam.html>.

Experimental

In a 50 ml Erlenmeyer flask dissolve 2.8 g of hydroxylamine HCL and 4 g of sodium acetate trihydrate in 12 ml of water. Warm the solution to 35-40 °C. To the warm mixture add 2.8 g of cyclohexanone. **What happened?** Stopper the flask and shake vigorously for two minutes. Cool the flask to room temperature and collect the product via vacuum filtration. Wash the product with cold distilled water (2 x 5 ml) and allow it to air dry over night. Perform analysis on formed product.

Place 1 g of formed product and 2 ml of sulfuric acid (80 %) in a 50 ml beaker. Heat the mixture on a hot plate in the hood until the reaction occurs (2-5 min). **What do you observe?** Cool the reaction mixture to room temperature, then in a sodium chloride ice-bath for ten minutes. Slowly add 50 % ammonium hydroxide solution while stirring until the solution becomes basic (**What pH?**) keeping the temperature below 20 °C (remember adding a base to an acid will produce heat). Add 15 ml of diethyl ether to the mixture and separate the two phases. Extract the aqueous layer with an additional 10 ml of diethyl ether. Dry the combined organic layer with anhydrous sodium sulfate. Decant the organic liquid into a clean Erlenmeyer flask and then concentrate on a sand bath to yield the product. Allow it to cool to room temperature, and then perform the necessary analysis.

Computational Chemistry (Spartan 2008 Molecular Model Program)

1. Construct a model of the intermediate(s) and the product.

2. Perform energy calculations, IR, and NMR.

3. Compare the energies between the possible intermediates.

4. Determine the percent difference of the calculated and experimental IR.

Waste Disposal

Collect all organic waste in a beaker during the experiment and dispose the combined waste at the end of the period into the **organic waste container inside the HOOD**.

Write-up

Follow the directions given in the syllabus.

Experiment 15
Synthesis of Caprolactam

Name: _____

Prelab Exercise : Provide the missing structures and their names in the above chemical equation.

Experiment 15

Name: ——

Answer the following questions:

1. Starting with Cyclohexane, outline a synthesis for the formation of the final compound that you synthesized.

2. Provide a detailed reaction mechanism for the second part of the experiment.

Synthesis of a Substituted Benzoic Acid

Purpose

The objective of this experiment is to determine the product formed from electrophilic aromatic substitution of benzoic acid. The intermediate will then undergo Fischer esterification reaction to yield the final product. At the end of the experiment, you will perform the following analysis (IR, ^{1}HNMR and MP) to confirm the identity of the reaction products.

Chemical Equation

Prelab Exercise : Give the chemical structures and the IUPAC names for the missing structures above.

Experimental

Warning : Sulfuric acid and nitric acid are corrosive. Handle with care!!

1.   S.S. Stradling; C.L. Gage, J. Chem. Ed. 1985, 62(12), 1116-1117.

Place 5 ml of concentrated sulfuric acid and a spin vane in a 25 mL Erlenmeyer flask and cool to 0 °C or less. **Keep cold.** Slowly add benzoic acid, 2.0 g to the flask and keep solution below 0°C. Add cold nitrating mixture (prepared from 2 ml of concentrated sulfuric acid and 1.34 ml of conc. nitric acid) **slowly** into the 25 ml Erlenmeyer flask. Cool the mixture to 0 °C or less, and keep **cold** for 15 minutes. Pour the cold mixture over 250 g of ice and stir vigorously until the ice melt. Collect the product by vacuum filter and wash with cold water (3 X 10 mL). Allow the product to air dry until next class period. Weigh the product and then perform MP and IR.

Place 1.0 gram of the intermediate, 8.0 ml of methanol, 0.4 ml of sulfuric acid, and spin vane into a 25 ml round-bottom flask. Attach a water condenser and then reflux for 1 hour. Pour the reaction mixture into an ice slurry (50 g ice and 10 mL water), stir the mixture and allowed the ice to melt. Collect the crude product by suction filtration, and then washed with water (3 X 5 mL). Allow the crude to dry. Recrystallize the crude from minimum amount of methanol. Rinse with cold methanol (2 X 5 mL) and then allow to air dry for 10 minutes. Weigh the product and the perform MP and IR.

Computational Chemistry (Spartan 2008 Molecular Model Program)

1. Construct a model of the intermediate(s) and the product.

2. Perform energy calculations, IR, and NMR.

3. Compare the energies between the possible intermediates.

4. Determine the percent difference of the calculated and experimental IR.

Waste Disposal

Collect all organic waste in a beaker during the experiment and dispose the combined waste at the end of the period into the **organic waste container inside the HOOD.**

Write-up

Follow the directions given in the syllabus.

Experiment 16
Synthesis of a Substituted Benzoic Acid

Name: —————————————————————————————————————

Prelab Exercise : Provide the missing structures and their names in this chemical reaction.

Experiment 16

Name: _____

Answer the following questions:

1. Starting with benzene, outline a synthesis for the formation of the final compound that you synthesized.

2. Provide a detailed reaction mechanism for the second part of the experiment.